DEDICATION

This book is dedicated to the young people of today who think that being thirty is old, forty is really old, and fifty is basically like having one foot in the grave.

I cherish your view of the world!

ACKNOWLEDGMENTS

(DON'T SKIP THIS LIKE YOU USUALLY DO!)

Before I acknowledge anything, or anyone else, I need to acknowledge The Light of Possibility. Your guidance is a lamp to my feet and a light to my path, as long as I follow The Light, I'm right where I need to be.

Other than The Light, I only want to acknowledge YOU, the reader of this book. You are the most important person in the world! I wrote this book, specifically for YOU!

You are the reason I wake up in the morning and write! You are the reason I am a life design expert! You are the reason for my passion and my purpose in life.

To me, you are the most important person in the world!

WHAT TO EXPECT IN THE ABC's OF SUCCESS

WARNING!

Whatever you do, DO NOT put this book down now that you have picked it up! This book can change your life!

If you read this book you are going to be happy, rich, better looking, and anything else you want to be in your life!

Okay, maybe that's not actually true. However, this book can in fact help you to live the exact life you want to live! Don't grow up to be an adult!

A
Dull
Unhappy
Life
Time

Stay young!

THE PROMISE

BEFORE WE GET STARTED, I NEED YOU TO MAKE YOURSELF A PROMISE.

THIS IS A SERIOUS PROMISE.

REPEAT AFTER ME:

I PROMISE, TO READ THIS ENTIRE BOOK!

I PROMISE, THAT I WILL NOT GIVE UP!

I PROMISE, THAT I WILL HAVE FUN!

I PROMISE TO ENJOY MY
JOURNEY OF BEING A TEENAGER!

_____

PLEASE SIGN YOUR NAME HERE.

1

HI! I'M TOM

Hey there! My name is Tom. I'm a life design expert, and it's my job to help people live the absolute best life they can. It's my job to show you how to imagine what could be possible for your life, and then show you how to turn your dreams into reality. It's the best JOB in the world, and if you want, I'll show you how to become one too!

Before we get started, I want to make you a BOLD PROMISE!

I promise that I can teach you how to be ANYTHING you want to be in your life. Literally anything!

I may not know you personally, and I may not know what you are going through or what you want to be, but that doesn't make any difference.

That's because I believe something. I believe, If you read this book, and apply the lessons to your life, you can live the most extraordinary life you've ever imagined.

I'm also pretty sure that some guy claiming he can help you is enough to make you doubt me right off the bat. All I'm asking for is a chance to prove myself to you. I only want to do one simple thing.

I want to help you live a better life than I did when I was your age!

Yes, compared to you, I'm old! In fact, right now I'm forty, which when I was your age basically meant I knew nothing, was just about dead, and was not the least bit cool. Okay, I'll agree with you on the not being cool part.

I'll actually even agree, and even insist on the part about not knowing anything, but I'm standing firm on the fact that I don't believe I'm just about dead. In fact, I feel more alive now than ever before. I know that sounds weird, but bear with me...

Here's what you need to know about me. I'm older than you, so by default I have to respect you, I was always taught to respect my youngers. I'm bigger than you, so I could probably take you in a fight, but I bruise easy so I won't attempt it, and besides, can't we all just get along?

Also, I'm bald because I want to be, NOT BECAUSE I'M OLD! When I was a young person, I loved my hair, and the thought of being bald scared me! Now, I can't stand hair, basically because it grows in places that hair shouldn't grow...like my ears! Gross!

What was I talking about again? Oh yeah...

Speaking of being a young person. I happen to have five of them. Yup, I'm a dad! I've managed to keep each and every one of them alive for their entire life so far..... (but the day isn't over yet!)

So why am I even writing this? Mostly, I'm writing this for my own kids, however, I figured since I was writing it anyway, I might as well give it to you too. Who knows? Maybe I'll say something that makes a difference in your life!

Here is the biggest reason I'm writing this book for you. I'm writing it because I seriously don't know anything! No, really, I don't. In fact, I'm so bad at doing what normal adults do, that I had to make up my own JOB!

I gave myself the title of "Life Design Expert." Because that's what I want to be.

The reality of my life is that I really had no idea what I wanted to be until very recently. Probably because there wasn't a "Job Title" that fit with my hopes, desires, and skills that I wanted to focus on.

I couldn't see myself doing something boring, day in, and day out. I didn't care as much about the money, as much as I cared about being excited and happy about what I was doing each day.

The other issue was that I didn't get a major degree from some big fancy school. I didn't even have the desire to go to college until I was in my last year of high school and found out that I could go to school for design. For me, the idea that I could actually do something I wanted to do because I wanted to do it never occurred to me. When that became an option, my entire outlook on education changed. Up until then, I was simply not a good student in the traditional educational system. Yet I excelled at creativity, art, and design because it mattered to me.

In fact, I almost didn't graduate high school because the teacher who taught me (okay, let me rephrase that, the teacher who graded me) to write, told me I wasn't good enough to go out into the "Real World" and get a job! She was right, which is why I created my own! Thanks teach! What's more, is that if it wasn't for spell check, and my mom who edits all my stuff, most of this would be spelled wrong.

What I realized was that what the rest of the world considered the "Real world" was not the world I wanted to devote myself to. I wanted to be part of a world that I was responsible for creating. I wanted to create a place of joy, happiness and personal success that had nothing to do with what the societal view of success was.

What I want you to understand is this. WHAT THE WORLD THINKS YOU ARE HAS NOTHING TO DO WITH WHO YOU WERE BORN TO BE!

You get to imagine, design, and create YOUR LIFE, and if anyone tells you that what you want isn't possible, then it's up to you to make it possible!

I believe in you, because I believe in possibility! To me, you are possibility! You are, quite possibly, the most extraordinary person I've never met. That doesn't stop me from believing in you though, because I believe that if you want to, you can change this world!

I believe a lot of things, but the older I get, the less I know. I've realized that what most of the adults in this world think matters, really has nothing to do with what does. I've realized that traditional education is important, but it's not as important as SELF EDUCATION! So I figured if I could write about what really matters in life, it would be like sticking my tongue out as Mrs. Whatserface.

As you read this book, I don't expect you to actually learn anything, so don't worry about that. I wouldn't want to be responsible for your brain.

3

If anything, I want one thing for you. I want this book to increase your belief in yourself and your ability to be anything you want to be in this world!

Just enjoy this book and use it as a way of designing the exact life you want to live. This is your life, you get one chance to live it, and life is too short to waste your moments! Man I can't stand old people statements like that!

Okay, I'll admit, technically I'm an adult because I'm old enough to be. For that reason alone I'll say things from time to time that will make you roll your eyes! When I was your age, I would have rolled mine too. If that happens, don't worry about it. Eye rolling is a normal symptom of being a teenager. You'll grow out of it.

As a final note, I want to encourage you to really do what this book asks you to do. If you don't, nothing will happen. Except that you won't be happier, better looking, and make more money than the person who does the work. That might not actually be true either.

Most of all….. Have fun, and whatever you do, don't learn anything, just discover!

2

Who am I?

You probably want to know who I am, and why anyone would even listen to what I have to say. Besides an old bald dude, I like to think that I'm a pretty normal guy. Who I am though, has nothing to do with being "Normal" or not. I am who I choose to be!

Who I choose to be is a happy, fun loving, positive guy who loves to help people (young people especially) to live their life with passion and purpose! That basically means that I believe you were born with a special and unique gift to offer this world, and it's my job to help you discover that gift. Once you discover that uniqueness about you, I believe that life takes on a whole new level of excitement and "Purpose" that brings something called "Passion" to your life.

I have to tell you though, I didn't always know who I am. It took me a long time to figure it out, because I listened to a lot of people who didn't really know me, tell me what they thought was best for me. But that wasn't their fault. They were just doing what they were told to do, and in their mind, they were doing a good thing.

Most times, when I was a kid, when someone asked me what I wanted to be when I got older, I couldn't really answer that in a way that <u>they</u> wanted. I felt like they wanted me to know what job I wanted as a "career." The problem was, I looked at what most adults were doing, and almost threw up because the idea of doing something so boring with my life made me sick!

Secretly, and I wasn't even sure if this is a job title, I wanted to just be

HAPPY! Well, I'm happy to tell you, it is a job title and in this book, I'm going to show you why!

Sure, when I was a kid, I wanted MONEY! Basically, because I personally didn't have any. My parents seemed to have some money, but that was theirs, and they weren't letting me have nearly enough of it! Plus, they always said "Sorry, we just don't have the money for that….."

So I thought "If I want to be happy, but I also want to have money, I need to figure out how to make money for being happy." I'm excited to tell you, that after many, many, (okay fine, many, many, many) years, I discovered the secret for being happy, and making money. Want to know what it is?

Keep reading!

3

Who you are

I don't have to ask who you are, because I already know! You are an absolutely amazing, awesomely talented, truly gifted individual who can have the very best that life has to offer! That is what I believe about you!

Sure, I may not know you personally, but when I think about you, I can honestly say that the very fact that you are reading this right now, makes you a freak of nature! Seriously, you are able to look at a page of black lines and figure out what they mean. That's just cool! Think about it.... No other creature on earth can do that!

You are so incredible that you might even doubt that you could be as awesome as I say you are. You are so perfect, so flawless, so good looking, so smart, and so likeable that I have a tear in my eye thinking about how proud I am of you. You ROCK!

Are you feeling good about yourself yet? I hope so! Because again, that's my job. But here is the secret I wanted to tell you.

I'm going to use my sly, whispery voice now, so make sure you read it that way......

Before I tell you the secret, make sure that no adults are listening. We wouldn't want them to know that you are smarter than them, especially after you hear this.

Are you in a super secret location? Good, here you go.

I'll fill you in on something that no one may have ever told you before. Your job in life is not what you do for a paycheck. Your job is not that boring thing adults do for hours every day and then come home and complain about. Your job in life is not what defines who you are.

Your Job in life is your **J**ourney **O**f **B**eing! Your J.O.B. in life is to BE YOU! So this book is all about Your Journey Of Being YOU! It's your J.O.B. to figure out who you are, what YOU want to do with YOUR LIFE, and then go out into this world and MAKE A DIFFERENCE!

4

What about the money

Make a difference? Didn't I say I would teach you how to make money?

Actually, I did tell you that I discovered the secret to being happy and making money. And here is the secret. There is NO secret! In fact, everything you have ever wanted to know about making money and being happier than anyone else is going to be spelled out in this book. Making money is the easy part, just go to work.

Being happy is the easy part too. Just choose to be happy.

Does that sound to simple for you? Perhaps it's because you've been taught that life isn't that simple. Maybe you see the adults around you, unhappy, not having the money they wish they had, and you don't want to be anything like them. I couldn't agree more!

I think one of the worst tragedies that ever occurred in life, is the moment when someone chooses to be unhappy. We'll get into that later in this book, but for now, just believe this.

Being happy in life is far more important than all the money in the world. Being personally successful in life is far more important than all the money in the world. Being who you truly want to be is far more important than all the money in the world. Being alive, and appreciating the life journey you are on is far more important than all the money in the world!

The real key to success is to grow successful on the inside, and then take that success out into the world so people see how valuable you are!

So for now, can I just ask you a favor? Will you allow me to teach you the secrets of life, that you probably aren't being taught anywhere else? If you will do that, then I will teach you the secret to living a life that is more rewarding and joyful than anything you can possibly imagine!

If you agree to that, then keep reading. If you don't, then stop here. Life is about to get interesting!

5

My Friend Frank

Much like you, I have a best friend. We met when I was 11 years old. He walked on to the school bus, asked if he could sit next to me, and from that day on, we were best friends for over twenty five years!

I couldn't even imagine being friends for that many years when I was your age, because I wasn't exactly sure how people even lived to be that old. That was like finding a fossil if you asked me.

But, much like your life, the next year, then five years, then ten and twenty years happened without me even knowing it. And when I was thirty six years old, and Frank was too, just eight days after his birthday in fact, FRANK DIED!

That's right, at just thirty six years old, my best friend died. I had grown up with him, we played ball together, went to school together and started families together. But now he was gone.

He left behind two little girls, Grace and Addison, who loved their daddy very much. He loved his daughters more than anything in the world, but now, he couldn't hug them anymore, and they couldn't hug him. This was a sad day and one where nobody chose to be happy. Because we were all sad.

If you have ever lost a friend or family member, you know how that feels and I'm sorry you have experienced the loss of a loved one. I've cried too, and I miss my best friend every day.

I want to tell you the happy part of that story though. Frank's death, gave me life!

Do you remember when I used the words "Passion" and "Purpose" a few chapters ago? Well, when Frank died, he gave me that as a gift. Whether he sent it down from above, or not, I believe that my passion for life, and my purpose of writing was a direct result of his death.

I began to realize how important every moment of our lives is. In fact, just imagine you were only going to live to be thirty six years old! How old are you now? Subtract your age from thirty six, and that would be how many years you have left to truly live life. Kind of a reality check huh?

You see, Frank had a lot of money before he died. But I am confident, that despite what he had, he would have given every single bit of it up, for one more day on earth.

Here is a bit of his story....

6

Frank's Story

When Frank and I met, He was just like me, An 11 year old kid, with one thing on his mind, being happy!

We did our job well as kids. We played, we explored, we got in trouble, and we repeated! We remained friends through high school, and even though we went to separate colleges, we still stayed friends. It was after college that both of our stories really started. I'm going to focus on Frank's story, because mine is boring compared to his.

After he finished college, Frank began working for a small company doing what he went to school for. It was pretty cool actually. He would travel a lot, and he got to meet big time celebrities and pro athletes.

He loved his job, and within about 10 years, he got to be a big shot in the company and was making a TON of money. And yes, I do mean a TON.

But one day he called me. He told me he had left the company, and wanted to discover what his true calling was in life.

I WAS SHOCKED!!!

For years, I had been totally jealous of Frank's success, and I thought that he had everything I wanted. He seemed to love his job, he made tons of money, and he had a wife, a dog, a huge house with a fence, fancy cars, and a ride on lawn mower! Man, I thought he had it all!

On the other hand, I seemed to be struggling to pay the bills, had a beat up old minivan that smelled like French fries, and was living in a two bedroom apartment with my wife and four kids. Do the math, the bedrooms don't work out!

So during that phone call, I discovered something about our lives. After college, Frank focused on his career and making money, while I focused on being happy with whatever life gave me, and began learning about something called....

PERSONAL DEVELOPMENT

I know, that sounds like something similar to a mushy dark green vegetable that is now cold and your parents are still forcing you to eat it.

However, personal development for me was like a secret super food that gave me more energy than anything I've ever consumed. It looked as though it tasted like barf to some people, but I knew that it tasted like swiss chocolate cotton candy. I would devour it like I hadn't eaten in days, every time I got a new book on a subject I loved. I began to realize that I could learn what I wanted to understand about life.

Personal development taught, what I wanted to learn!

It was the first time in my life that I realized that I could direct the path of my life through the way I thought.

I thought, "WOW, I could be a super hero and my power would be mind control....COOL! Give me more please!"

When Frank told me he was leaving his job to find his "Passion" and live his "Purpose" I realized that he wasn't as happy with his job as I thought he was. In fact, he told me that the money didn't even matter to him. He said he would rather be doing something he truly felt joy from doing.

I was beginning to realize something!

7

The beginning

Frank died two years after that phone call. You might wonder why I called this the beginning, when for him, it was the end. And I'll tell you exactly why.

You see, when frank died, it made me realize something. I needed to begin doing what mattered to me in my life before it was my turn to go. When I realized that I had what Frank didn't, which was inner joy, and Frank had what I didn't, which was outer success, I began to think.

"How could I use what I have learned, to create something that would allow me to do what I love to do, and make money from it?"

That was my light bulb moment!

One thing was clear to me though. I needed to do what I love to do, far more than I needed to make money from it. Frank taught me that lesson, because I believe that Frank would give up everything he ever had, for one more day on earth.

The problem was, I had no idea what I wanted to do!

I did realize one thing though. I had been studying personal development for over twenty years, and it had made a huge difference in my life. What I really wanted to do was write down everything I had learned over my years of life, and leave it behind as a sort of "how to" manual for my kids.

That's when I began writing. But don't get it twisted, I didn't start writing as a way of making money. I began doing it because it was what I wanted to do.

Ding, Ding, Ding!!!! Did you hear that? If not, WAKE UP! I'm talking here!

I know I can get boring, it's what old folks do. But sometimes I might say something that I believe can make a huge difference in your life. So pay attention, or at least pretend to be interested.

When I say "Don't get it twisted," it's not just an eye rolling attempt at doing my best to sound relevant. It's something I really need you to understand.

You see, I began to write because I felt an inner drive, a calling, or a desire to do it. I realized that if I didn't have money, or cars, or houses to leave to my children, I at least wanted to leave them with my words of advice.

That might sound lame. You might be disappointed if you expected to get wealthy from someone who dies and leaves you everything in his will, but he only leaves you a book. Yet, what if, within the pages of that book was a clue to all the joy, happiness, success, and money you could ever desire, and all you had to do was realize that what he was saying to you was the treasure map.

But what if, out of disappointment, you never opened the book to discover that map? The whole time, you wished you were left with something of "Value" and something that was actually worth something, and all you had was a book.

That is what I realized I wanted to leave my children. I wanted to leave them something that most people don't. The information in my head! The years it took me to learn what I am teaching you now are that treasure map to living a life that is more rewarding than all the money on earth!

Yes, you can use this information to make money when you get old enough too, if you want. However, my focus in this book is to help you understand that life is about a lot more than what you do, in order to have what you want. This book is about BEING YOU!

I'm talking about being who you were born to be and living life how it's supposed to be lived!

16

8

So what

So what are you actually going to get out of this book? Well, I believe you are going to get out of this book, exactly what you put into this book.

I hope, that this book is something you chose to read, and not something you were forced to read like some of those ridiculously boring stories they make you read in school sometimes. But if you were forced to read it, then I hope you will do something for yourself. Make the best of it!

Regardless of whether or not you are being threatened with lifetime grounding if you don't read this or if you picked it up and thought it looked like it was worth your time, just relax. Enjoy each chapter. And ask "How can I relate this to MY life?"

I've worked very hard to be interesting, relevant to your life, and (questionably) funny!

So then, what you believe you will get out of this book is probably what you will experience. If you think you will get nothing out of it, you'll hate it and it's just a waste of time, then that is what you'll probably get out of this book. That's basically how every situation works.

On the contrary, if you look at this book as a super cool, unique, fun way of thinking about what your life can be, then I think you will get a lot out of this book.

With that said, what exactly are you going to discover? Well, I'd like to think that you are going to discover exactly what you need to find, in order to be successful in EVERY area of your life.

By every area of your life, I mean, the areas of life that matter to you right now. I'm going to guess that those areas are your view of what is possible in your lifetime, your relationships, your education, being able to be happy, and what the future holds for you.

I probably missed a few, however, in general, I would say that we could categorize your life into those areas.

Specifically though, I'm going to teach you how to achieve ANY goal you want to achieve in life!

You see, it took me a lot of years to learn this stuff! And believe me If I knew at your age, what I know now, I wouldn't have wasted all those years struggling to get where I am today!

That one just might be the biggest eye roller in the whole book! But it's true!

9

On your mark

It's time to take your place and get ready for your journey!

Unlike a typical race however, there is no need to run this one. You can, and should, walk, enjoying each step of the journey. Your life, and every moment along the way is a gift to discover, hold, and appreciate.

Your experiences in this book, and in life, are going to be unique to you. I encourage you to share your experiences along the way, and here's how.

Use this book like a workbook. I'll post some questions, like this one:

QUESTION:

What is the number one thing you are hoping this book will do for you?

_____

_____

By writing in this book, and using the questions to help your brain begin to understand what it's supposed to be focused on, you'll begin to see results!

As you answer the questions, and learn each lesson (okay, I'm sorry, I lied…you might actually learn something) pay close attention to how using the lesson is helping you in your life.

Keep in mind!
You are just learning this stuff. So if it doesn't seem to be working right away

DON'T GIVE UP!!!

You might mess up, but don't give up! If I can give you one simple piece of advice before you close this book and ignore me for the rest of your life, that would be it.

MESS UP – JUST DON'T GIVE UP!

If you only want to know the simplest idea I have, that would be it. So if that's all you wanted, then you can stop reading now.

But if you want to learn some more stuff that can benefit you… keep reading!

10

Get Set

Okay, since you are still reading, I'm willing to bet that you are ready to learn some stuff that may (Or may not) help you live the rest of your life in an extraordinary way! I'm excited about that, because otherwise I would have written this for no reason, other than to hear myself talk, and to be honest, I've heard what I have to say already...

So I'm glad you're still listening. I've got some more bad jokes, horribly old guy stuff to say, and to be perfectly honest with you, this is about my only talent. So I'll keep typing. I learned how to do it high school so I might as well use it for something.

This first section of the book is called "The ABC's Of Success!"

There are a couple reasons I call them the ABC's. First, they are basic and simple. In fact, I don't like complicating things, it just makes them ...... well ...... complicated.

So if it's okay with you (okay the real reason is because I'm not that smart) I'm going to keep this book simple, fun, and moving along quickly. Cool?

Alright good!

So if you are ready to get started, I'd like to ask you another question.

"What do you want to be?"

NOOOOOO!!!! Not in the dreaded, classic, most boring adult question ever asked kind of way!!!

I honestly don't have much concern right now for what you want to be when you get older. I want to know what you want to be RIGHT NOW!!

Maybe not right now, but perhaps in the not so distant future.

When I ask, "What do you want to be?" I'm asking for something like this:
"I want to be better at baseball."
"I want to be getting better grades."
"I want to be the best cheerleader on my team."

These are called "Short Term Goals" and they are what you can use this book to work on.

So go ahead, and without worrying about it too much, just think of something that matters to you and write it down. You'll have a chance to set more, and even bigger goals later on. For now....
Keep your goal simple and go ahead and write one down now!

It's best to be specific about your goal, however, as you are getting started, the most important thing is to put your pen to the page and begin writing down goals.

Go for it!

"I want to be

_____ "

11

GO!

It's time to take your first step, on Your Journey Of Being A Teenager!

By that, I mean it's now time to accept your fate and begin embracing the fact that you were born to be an extraordinary person who can accomplish anything you want in your life! I'm going to give you the tools, knowledge, and encouragement to do it! It's up to you however, to DO THE WORK!

I know! I know…Nobody said anything about work!!

But wait! Before you close this book, the work I'm talking about is FUN work. It's like that favorite project you get to do because it's actually a fun assignment. It doesn't seem like work, it doesn't feel like work, and it certainly doesn't appear like you are learning anything in the process. But somehow you do!

Sneaky right…

So that is what I'm asking of you! Just have fun! DO the work, and ENJOY THE PROCESS!

I have seen this stuff work in people a lot less smart than you, a lot less good looking than you, and a lot less impressed with me than you are right now. Try to contain your laughter please, you're embarrassing me!

The truth is, if you stop wondering what the result will be, and you enjoy the process, your ability to really appreciate life as it's happening will take

23

your life to new heights! That's called peak performance!

I'm going to teach you how to reach the peak, you just need to follow me, step where I step, and enjoy the journey. Trust me, I've been where you are before!

Okay, maybe I don't know exactly where you are, or what you may be dealing with. I also understand that you might be dealing with some pretty tough stuff right now. So all I am going to require of you is trust. I know I have to earn that, and I'm hoping that I'm starting to. As long as I haven't lost any yet, I'm willing to work with that!

Trust me, trust the process, and trust your own ability!

Realistically,
Every
Single
Person
Earns
Certain
Trust

If you respect the fact that I am here to respect you for who you are, then we can get started with a mutual respect for each other!

I'm not here to pretend to know it all. In fact, I would bet that if we sat down together, you could help me to discover a few things about life that I didn't understand.

For now, since you are where you are, and I'm where I am, just allow me to pour into you, what I believe to be the most valuable and useful information I've ever shared.

If that changes your life in some way, for the better, then I will have done my job well.

12

The ABC's

I know you are smart. I don't doubt that for one single second! So don't confuse the fact that I keep things simple, with a disbelief of your ability to handle more complicated stuff.

The reason I keep things simple is because I believe that life should be simple. I also believe that if your life is complicated, you're not really living it the way it should be lived.

So If I can teach you simple ways of, well... simplifying life, then you can help those people who seem to complicate life by also teaching them some simple concepts. Together we can create a world that is simpler to live in!

WOULDN'T THAT BE AWESOME!

Back to the question. What do you want to be?

I'm going to ask that you write down the answer to that question now. Instead of just one answer, let a few things that you want to be, come out. Just let it flow.

"What do you want to be?"

"Well Tom, let me tell you..... I want to be,

_____

_____ "

Great, now I can teach you how to BE IT!

The first thing you need to understand about life is that nothing happens without ACTION! It's the "A" in The ABC's Of Success! They yell it before they do anything in Hollywood, because they are producing something like a movie.

If you want to produce results in your own life, then you too need to take "ACTION!"

This is your life, and it's time to start taking action on producing, directing, and playing your part!

Imagine if your life was a movie. What role would you want to play? What characters would you want to include in your story? What would the soundtrack be? What would the environment look like?

These might sound like things that are out of your ability to control, however, you get to choose everything in your life. We'll get more into that later. For now, just think about what types of actions you would need to take in order to "Be what you want to be!"

For now, remember this

"Change Happens At The Level Of Action!"

Everyone wants things in their life. The people that get what they want are the ones who take action. For instance, if you wanted to be 10 pounds lighter, your action might be to exercise with the focus on losing weight for a half hour. Or if you wanted to be working at a specific career, you could write to the companies you want to work for and ask what they recommend you focus on learning. Perhaps you want to be playing with a new electronic device that your parents won't buy for you. You could write down ways to begin earning some money to buy it yourself.

What are some actions you could take that will move you closer to what you want to be? Write them down now!

_____

_____

The "B" in the ABC's is your BELIEF!

I love the word belief! I love what belief can do for us. I do believe that I love belief more than anything. And yes, maybe I will marry it and live happily ever after......

Belief is the foundation of everything you do in life. When I draw this out for you, you'll see how belief is always at the bottom of everything you do. If you build your life upon a solid belief system, you can reach infinite levels of success!

What happens to a lot of those crabby old adults (oops, did I say that out loud?) is that when they are growing up, they don't build on a solid foundation, so their lives begin to sort of crumble.

That's typically why so many people grow up to live lives of quiet desperation, longing for something better, and generally unhappy with what their life has become. That's sad! In fact, I'm going to give it a sad face emoji :(

What I mean by that, is how you probably see lots of adults and wonder why they seem unhappy. It's not that they are unhappy with their whole life, it's because they believe that their life is not what it's supposed to be.

Too many people long for a better life, wish they were luckier, and even though they won't admit it, wish they learned this stuff at your age.

You don't know how easy you have it! When I was your age, we didn't have this stuff. Youth is wasted on the young!

Oh, I can HEAR your eyes rolling right now! And I LOVE IT!!!

I believe it's time to change the way young people think about life. I believe it's time that you begin learning what truly matters in life, and that is exactly why I am writing this book.

I want to be the person who is responsible for you never saying to your kids one day (EWW, what, that might happen?) "When I was your age, we didn't have this stuff." BECAUSE YOU DO!!!!

Personally, I'm out to change education so that every young person learns how to pursue their passion and purpose in life as if it was the most important aspect of your life!

So based on my belief of that being possible for you, I would need to believe things like:

"I believe it's possible to alter the direction of the world and help people live better lives!"

"I believe people want to improve their lives and I believe I can help them do it!"

Now that you know some of the beliefs I have, what would you have to believe in order to be what you want to be? Maybe you would need beliefs like:

"I believe that I can be anything I want to be!"

"I believe I can get a 100% on my test!"

"I believe I will get that job!"

"I believe I can do a back handspring!"

"I believe in my ability to work at Disney!"

"I believe that girl will say yes to going out with me!"

Go ahead and write down <u>what you want to believe</u> right now:

"I believe

_____

_____

_____

_____

_____

The "C" in the ABC's is your consistency! My mom always said that consistency is the hardest word we ever learn. It's not hard to say or spell, it's just hard to do anything......consistently.

Consistency is the factor in the success equation that is the hardest to figure out. That's because LIFE GETS IN THE WAY!

The most successful people in the world find a way to make life work around what matters to them. Unsuccessful people work what matters to them around their life.

What I mean by that is how many people say "I just don't have the time...." When in reality, we do have the time, it's just a matter of using your time effectively. I'll talk more about that when we discuss time management.

What I want you to understand about consistency can be summed up in the story of "The Tortoise and the hare!"

Have you ever noticed how a lot of people (Not you of course) start something and then stop a short time later? They put a TON of energy into it the first few days or weeks, and then they burn out.

They actually do have the right belief, and they do take the right actions, but when it comes to being consistent for the amount of time it takes to succeed, that's when it all starts to crumble.

In the story of the tortoise and the hare, the hare is running really fast, then he takes a nap. He takes off again, tires out, and takes another nap.

The tortoise understands that if he remains consistent, he will reach the goal. He also gets to enjoy the journey, appreciate the view, and laugh at the hare who is trying too hard.

On the journey of life, be a tortoise! Be consistent!

How often would you have to do the actions you need to do, and how often would you need to believe what you need to believe?

Sometimes, that is EVERY DAY! And if that is true, then don't let life get in the way, stay consistent.

Go ahead and write down how consistently you need to be doing what you need to be doing.

I need to consistently do my actions, and focus on my beliefs, at these times:

_____

_____

As you begin to learn this concept, I want you to envision (vividly imagine) that every goal you want to achieve is like climbing a mountain. What you want is at the peak.

So basically, whenever you want something in your life, you are on a journey of "BEING" it. The goal is at the peak of the mountain, and you begin your journey in the same place each time.

Some of your journeys will take you a very long time, and some of your journeys will not. Some of them will be easy, and others will be difficult. Some of your goals will be achieved successfully, other times you may fall short of reaching the peak.

As long as you understand that each of the things you want to be in your life, is its own unique journey of being (job) then you are already doing an amazing job of creating your life, the way you want to live it!

When you use the ABC's of Success to plan your goals, it will look like this.

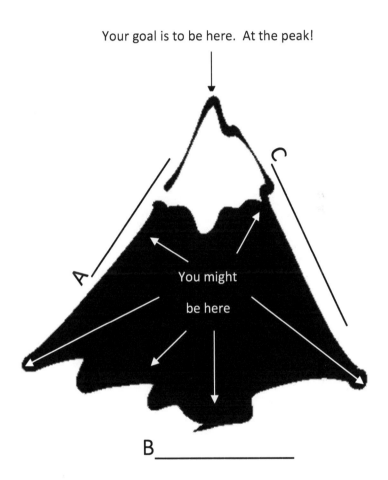

Your goal is to be here. At the peak!

C

A

You might

be here

B_____

Go ahead and write in the words that go with the ABC's.

No matter where you believe you are, on your journey of being what you want to be, just accept where you are and be okay with it!

I promise, I'll show you how to reach the peak, and be exactly where you want to be!

13

Use your Head

Have you ever considered exactly what goes on in that head of yours? I mean seriously, think of all the things your brain is capable of doing! From solving problems, to being creative, and learning all types of new stuff each day. You are one smart cookie! Why do adults say that? Cookies aren't even smart?

Anyway, here is something that you might not know. Your brain is like a mini computer. Just like a computer, it only knows what you tell it. Sure, it comes pre-programmed with certain abilities, but in order for it to work at its fullest potential, it needs information. But here is something really cool about your computer like brain.

Your brain does not know the difference between what is real, and what YOU tell it!

HUH?

What do I mean by that? I'll give you an example. If you tell your brain that you like something, it believes it. If you tell your brain that you don't like something, it believes that too.

If you tell your brain that you CAN do something, your brain believes what you tell it. And if you tell your brain that you can't do something, then your brain has no choice but to believe it.

Your brain cannot tell the difference between what is real and what you tell it.

Understand?

If not, just remember this:

Whatever you want to believe, that is what you need to be saying to yourself. We're going to talk more about this in a bit.

Okay, I need to tell you about a really bad four letter word. If you're not allowed to say "Bad" words, then keep reading! I'm going to give you a word that is worse than any other bad word. In fact, it's so bad, it turns itself into four words so it's even worse!

Cover your ears if you aren't allowed to hear bad words either, because here it comes....

C.A.N.T

Can't! Oh, the horror of it all!

Why is that such a bad word? I'll tell you. When you use the word can't, you eliminate something called possibility. During our time together, I want to help you to believe that ANYTHING IS POSSIBLE!

Okay sure, I understand that you turning into an elephant right now isn't exactly "Possible," however, I don't like to say that anything is impossible because if it did happen, I would be wrong, and I don't know about you, but I don't like being told I'm wrong. So let's just agree that anything really is possible, and if we agree on that, neither of us ever has to be wrong about anything!

Alright, back to the point.

The word can't is a Disempowering word. When someone "Disses" someone else, they tell them things that don't "Empower" them. They DISrespect that person. They DISempower them, and they DISillusion them.

If anything really is possible, until they DISprove it, it remains possible. Even if they do DISprove it, it doesn't make it impossible, it just means their perspective is possible.

So for instance, someone might say "You can't do that!" I'm sure you've heard that before right? Yet, is that true?

So what is the first of the four words that C.a.n.t. turns into?

The "C" in the word can't is Can't. So basically what I am saying is that you should not use the word can't, in a disempowering way. I'm not saying you can't use the word can't, because it can also empower you if you use it correctly.

The "A" in can't is ALWAYS!

Have you ever been talking to someone, and they say "You ALWAYS do that!" Well, always is another word that eliminates possibility. If something always happens, then the ability for it not to happen no longer exists.

So let me give you an example of how you might use Can't and always in a disempowering sentence.

"I can't _____ because _____

always _____!""

Fill in the blanks and let me know if you feel empowered?

I'm going to guess that because you are smart, that you can see what is happening here. Yet there is a third word we haven't talked about yet.

The "N" in c.a.n.t. is NEVER! Never, Never, Never.....

Never is another word that eliminates possibility. Here is an example of how you might use this word improperly.

"I CAN'T _____, because _____

ALWAYS _____ and _____

NEVER _____...."

Or, how about when someone says it to you!

"YOU can't _____, because

YOU always _____ and

YOU never _____."

Yuck! I'm getting disgusted just saying these words and I hope you are too!

Now for the final word. The "T" in can't is the word TRY.

So why shouldn't you use the word try? After all, aren't you trying to do something when you give it a shot? Aren't you trying to hit the ball or get good grades? You are, however, there is a key to success that I want you to understand right now.

Trying, doesn't actually exist. To illustrate this point, place this book down right now with the pages open so you can still read this.

Okay, now try to turn the page. Go ahead and do it now. Try to turn the page.

Did you do it? If you did, then you didn't try, you did it. If you didn't do it, then you didn't do it. You either do, or you do not. There is no trying. Thanks for that, Yoda.

So from now on, instead of using the word "Try" I would like you to instead say "I will do my best!"

Each of those four words can actually be used to empower you as well!

For instance, you can say:
"I can't stop because this matters to me!"
"I always achieve what I set my mind to do!"
"I never stop or give up on my goals!"

So how can you use the word "Try?" For yourself, I hope you don't. Again, I want you to remember that you don't try, you DO YOUR BEST!

However, for your friends, who haven't read this book, you can be encouraging and empowering to them by saying "Give it a try!" This is going to encourage them, and secretly you'll know that you are using a Jedi mind trick on them to get them to DO IT!

Alright, now that you understand the four most disempowering words you should never use, I want to introduce you to the two most powerful words you can use to become anything you want to become.

I'll go slow because it might take a while to learn how to spell these words. The first is "I." Take your time, I know this can be difficult for some.

The next word is "AM." It's okay, don't panic! I won't test you on the spelling!

Write them down here for practice _____

How can these two little words be so powerful? It's because, again, your brain doesn't know the difference between what is real and what you tell it.

If you tell your brain "I am ABLE" Your brain believes it.

If you tell your brain "I am NOT able" then your brain believes that too.

Your brain is only capable of believing and doing what you tell it to believe and do. It's just like a computer, IT MUST BE PROGRAMMED!

So I want to encourage you to choose your last words very carefully. Wait, isn't that what they say before they execute people?

Okay, I hope you are never in that situation! What I mean is that whatever you choose as the words that follow "I am" are going to tell your brain what it believes you are, or are not.

Right now, think of that goal you set for yourself. What would you have to believe, in order to achieve that goal? Now, go ahead and write some "I am" statements that empower that belief.

I am _____

I am _____

I am _____

Awesome job!

What you did is called, writing affirmations. To affirm something is to "State it as a fact." And the suffix, "ation," means to cause a result because of an action.

So when you state an "I am" affirm-ation, you state a fact that causes your brain to believe it.

Now that you understand that fact, I hope it causes extraordinary results in your life because you chose to take action!

Remember, ACTION is the "A" in the ABC's and change happens at the level of action!

More than anything, I want you to understand that it's not always what you say, it's how you say it, that makes a huge difference in your life. You'll understand this more as you progress in this book.

Let's keep going!

14

Put the SMACK Down

I'm going to teach you some super top secret techniques that are going to allow you to put the smack down on life.

Have you ever noticed how a lot of adults seem beat up by life? They look beat up, they sound defeated, and they limp around like zombies just doing their best to make it through each day of work.

If you have, then I need to teach you how to avoid something called "Zombieism!"

At the very least, I need to teach you how to put the smack down on life itself so that you don't let life bite you in the butt and turn you into a zombie!

By putting the smack down, I'm saying that I want to teach you how to tell life the way it's going to be. Most adults tend to be what is called "Reactive" to life. Which means they "React" to their situations.

I want to teach you how to be "Proactive" to life. Which means that you will be able to "Create" life the way you want it to be!

Remember, this is YOUR JOURNEY OF BEING!

So before you do anything in life, the very first thing I need to teach you, is HOW TO BE!

You are a human being. So with that said, I want to introduce you to a specific pattern of achieving and getting what you want out of life.

Here is the pattern:

Be ------ Do ------- Have -------

Whatever you want to have in life, requires you to follow this pattern in order to live that life.

So first, you must BE what it takes. This all starts with your BE-lief. What you BE-lieve you are, you BE-come! By writing down, and consistently telling yourself the "I AM" statements that you want your brain to believe, you begin to BE that in your life.

Then, once you BE-gin, to BE-come, what you BE-lieve is possible, then you must DO.

You must DO what it takes in order to HAVE what you want. The DO-ing is what occurs with the actions. When you are DO-ing what it takes, based on what you BE-lieve, and you do it consistently enough, then you will HAVE the life you CREATE!

This goes for EVERYTHING in life! You are either creating the life you DO want, or you are creating the life you DON'T want.

OUCH! Could you really be responsible for your life? I'm afraid so my friend.

Do you ever hear adults complaining about their "Situations" in life, but don't see them doing anything to change it? That is because they are BEING reactive, instead of proactive.

So how do you put the smack down on your life, your goals, and the zombies out there who just seem to drag their feet?

Once again, I'm going to use an ACRONYM!

An acronym is a group of letters that helps you remember an advanced concept.

S . M . A . C . K . is an acronym.

I use them because they are fun, and for some reason, they just come to me. It's a gift!

Now, since you are a young person, you're whole life can be lived by these exact principles that you are learning. To clarify what I mean by goals, I'll say this.

Anything you want to be in your life is a goal.
Anything you want to do in your life is a goal.
Anything you want to have in your life is a goal.

Since you know the pattern is be, do, have, you first have to BE. So that is what I am going to focus on teaching you in regards to goal setting. The word BE.

Just because a goal is also something you want to do or have, does not mean you need to phrase it differently. This is because you are always "Being" or "Not Being" something.

For instance. If you want to have money, you need to BE earning money. If you want to HAVE a job, you need to BE working. So when phrasing your goals, always ask "What do I want to be?"

Let's practice….

I want to be _____

I want to be _____

I want to be _____

Great! Now let me ask you a very important question. If I looked at your goal, would I know exactly what you wanted to be?

The reason I ask, is because that is the first thing you need to BE in order to put the smack down on your goals.

The "S" in smack, stands for being SPECIFIC.

Is what you want to be, very specific? For instance, a specific goal is not "I want to be a good student." However, a specific goal is "I want to be earning all A's on my next report card."

So if your goals were not specific enough the last time you wrote them down, then go ahead and clarify them now, or just write a few more.

I want to be _____

I want to be _____

I want to be _____

Now that you are SPECIFIC about what you want to be, I want to ask you another question.

Do your goals MOTIVATE you?

The "M" in smack, is that you must BE motivated! The only way to motivate yourself to the level you need to be, in order to achieve your goals, is to know WHY you are doing it. Your reason why is going to motivate you, or not motivate you. Your reason why NEEDS TO MOTIVATE YOU!

So let's practice this. Pick one of your goals and make it the first thing you want to achieve. Now fill in the blanks.

The reason why I want to be

_____

Is because

_____

_____

Are you motivated by your reason why?

Good!

The next thing you need to BE is ACHIEVING steps toward your goal consistently. They can be small steps, as long as you are achieving them consistently. Once you stop achieving steps toward your goal, you get stopped.

BIG goals in life, accomplished, are nothing more than a series of little goals, achieved, along the way. You can break down any goal into a smaller goal and when you accomplish it, that goal takes you to a new level of success!

The only way to achieve any goal is to take each specific step toward the top. For instance, perhaps you want to be on a specific sports team in your school. Here are some "Steps" you could take to accomplish that goal.

I want to be on the _____ team:

Step one - decide what position I would be best suited for.

Step two - look on youtube for examples of achieving in that position.

Step three - find a parent, relative, or friend who is knowledgeable about that position, who could spend time helping me practice and talk to them about it.

Step four - investigate what exercises would help me strengthen the muscles that would help me perform the best.

Step five - spend time practicing on my own each day for 1 hour.

Step six - commit to incorporate all of these steps into my daily life.

So based on your goal, what are the steps you need to take, in order to be achieving what it takes to accomplish the larger goal?

Step one _____

Step two _____

Step three _____

Excellent work!

You are well on your way to being a goal setting genius, and being proactive about your life. You can have as many steps as you need in order to achieve any goal. Let's move on!

Each step you take moves you one step closer to your goal of being what you want to be. Just like climbing a real mountain, your climb to the top of your success mountain is taken step by step.

Make no mistake though, sometimes, those steps may be scary to take. You may be tired, you may be unsure of where to step, and you may feel like you won't reach the peak. Let me assure you, I'm going to give you EVERYTHING you need to reach the peak.

In "THE NEXT LEVEL" which is the second book in this series, I will teach you how to overcome the four things that will attempt to stop you from being who you want to be in your life.

For now, I need you to just understand one thing. It's the "C" word in smack. Committed! YOU MUST BE COMMITTED!

Being committed comes from your reason why as well. It's the reason WHY achieving this goal MATTERS to you.

So WHY does achieving this goal MATTER to you?

This goal MATTERS to me because

_____

_____

Now we have a SPECIFIC goal, and that goal MOTIVATES you to take steps to ACHIEVE that goal. You are COMMITTED to accomplishing that goal because your reason why really matters to you.

What's left?

It's the most important of them all. If you don't do this, you will not reach the peak.

YOU MUST - KEEP GOING!!!!!

"K" Keep going.

You may get tired. You may feel like you "Can't" do it. You will likely come up against some obstacles along the way. Despite what happens during your climb to the peak, the only way to assure failure is to stop! You must keep going, no matter what!

Specific (Exactly what you are going to do)
Motivated (By your why)
Achieving (Step by step)
Committed (Because it matters to you)
Keep going (because you MUST)

If you follow this simple guide for setting, and achieving any goal, you will be well equipped to truly live the life you want to live. Many adults get STUCK, living the life they don't want to live because they haven't learned these things.

It's all REALLY SIMPLE, however, achieving your goals and living the life you want to live is NOT ALWAYS EASY!

There is a big difference between simple and easy. I'm going to teach you the simple ways of life, but I won't promise that your life will be easy just because you know this stuff.

I will say that, based on my experience, I have seen these methods work time and time again to help people around the world live simpler, happier, more successful lives.

So remember to BE what you need to be, and DO what you need to do, so you can HAVE what you want to have.

And put the SMACK down on life, before life has the chance to put the SMACK DOWN on you!

15

Time Machines

Wouldn't it be great if we had a time machine so if we ran out of time to do something we could just go back, adjust what we used our time for in the first place, and use our time more wisely!

Like, if you walked in to class and didn't have time to finish your homework yet, you could go back, not watch television, and do the work instead so it was done on time.

WELL...... unfortunately, that's not possible, yet.....

Until you get rich and famous by developing the first ever time machine, we're going to teach you how to get your work done before class.

But this isn't about homework. This section is about using the time you have, effectively, so that you accomplish what you want to in your lifetime.

Have you ever heard adults say "I don't have the time...." I know I have. I've even said it. Sometimes it may be true, but many times it's just a reason people use as a result of not using the time they do have.....effectively.

I've used that word twice now. Effectively. That word means to use in such a way that you achieve a desired result. Too many people use their time ineffectively, so they don't achieve their desired result.

As a young person, you probably don't worry about how much time you have left to live your life. At your age, I didn't either. In fact, it wasn't until my friend died when he was just thirty six (yes that's young in old people years) that time began to have significant importance to me.

You and I get the same amount of daily "Time," everyone does. We all get twenty four hours each day. UNTIL the day comes when that is no longer true. Don't get me wrong, I don't want you to worry about any of that stuff, because life is to be lived, in the moment, and every moment of life should matter to you!

This chapter is about something called Effective Time Management. The number one reason people use for not achieving their goals in life is "I don't have the time." There are a lot of others like, "I don't have the money, the skills, or the help…." And so on. There is one big difference between all of them though.

Money, skills, help, knowledge, and other "Reasons" can all be acquired. The one thing that cannot be acquired however is time. Time is universally the same for everyone. In fact, time doesn't actually exist in the way you may think it does.

Time is simply a way for us to measure the space between moments and when we need to meet at a particular moment, we use time as the reference point.

So if I say "Right now" the time is different for us all. But the moment is the same. The moment is right now, regardless of the time.

I guess what I'm saying is that I'm more interested in teaching you "Moment Management" than "Time Management."

Moments matter. We only get one moment, which is the one you are in right now! How you use this moment, and all the remaining moments of your life, is what adds up to your "Life Time!"

When people say they don't have the time, it's typically because what needs to be done doesn't really matter to them. If something matters, we find the time to do it. The problem is, many people don't have their priorities straight, and therefore, they don't know what matters to them. So they waste their time doing things that don't matter.

Because you are a young person, and you being concerned about time doesn't seem to be much of an issue for you, I'm going to give you one simple thing to remember.

Time is your most valuable treasure in life! Those who know what they want to be, write down the goals they want to achieve, and consistently use the moments they have effectively, go on to live the best lives.

I'll give you an example of how time adds up. If you took two hours each day and worked on something that truly mattered to you, instead of doing something that doesn't, you would give yourself thirty days of time this year! That's a whole month of additional time where you don't need to eat, sleep, or do anything else but focus on what matters to you.

Is that easy to do? No, of course not. However, for many people, if they were to add up the amount of time they spend on apps, social media, watching television, playing games, and doing other things that "waste their time" they would be surprised at how that time adds up.

Even if you just found one hour each day, you would still give yourself fifteen days of time, over two weeks of additional days, this year!

Is that still too much? How about 1 hour, three days per week? That's six days of time this year! Those hours, which are nothing more than a series of moments, add up to significant time.

Use your moments wisely!

You can also become more effective at "Moment Management" by using the seemingly small amounts of time you have. Each time you pop something in the microwave, rather than standing there waiting for the oven to ding, use that time to read a page of this book. Or to do a chore, or to do something else that needs to be done.

Seconds add up to minutes, then to hours, then to days, weeks, months, years and eventually your life time.

I would encourage you, starting right now, even at your age, to begin treasuring your time. It is your most valuable resource and your most precious gift.

Commit to using your time more effectively. Write down some ways you can be more effective at moment management.

_____

_____

I'll give you an example of "Moment Management."

Let's say that you get home from school and you, as usual, have homework, chores, and you need to practice your _____
(Instrument, sport, art, etc.....)

Because it's been a long day, you are tired, and you don't feel like it. Understandably, you grab a snack, sit down on the couch, flip on the television, and watch an hour of t.v.

Now, you begin playing the hot new game and before you know it, you realize it's just before your mom gets home. You know she is going to ask you if you have done your homework, chores, and practice. So you begin frantically racing through the house, doing your chores, you pull out your instrument to make it look like you were practicing, and you throw your books open on the table.

You know, you haven't used your moments effectively. So instead of being able to relax, enjoy the time with your mom, and have her be excited that you are the responsible person she is working hard to raise, you have to put on an act of being overwhelmed by your homework, chores, and practice because there just isn't "Enough time...."

She is disappointed, because she wishes she had more time to spend with you, but because things aren't done, she can't. She's frustrated, you're frustrated, and instead of having a nice evening together, there is tension.

Sound familiar?

You can probably relate this to your own life in some way. In fact, you can probably see how your mom, dad, family, friends, teachers, and many people do the same thing. They use time as an excuse because they don't manage it effectively. Here's why.

WE MAKE TIME FOR WHAT MATTERS!

So what would matter in this situation? That's for you to decide. Do you want tension, frustration, to act overwhelmed, and worry about getting in trouble for not doing what you needed to do? Probably not..

In order to use your time, and your moments, effectively, you need to decide what matters to you. In this case, I would use examples like this.

1. Having a relaxing evening with my mom matters to me.
2. Seeing my mom happy matters to me.
3. Helping around the house matters to me.
4. Getting my homework done matters to me.
5. Playing some games matters to me.
6. Watching some t.v. matters to me.
7. Practicing my instrument matters to me.

In reality, it all matters to you. It also matters to your mom. With the list above, you make it all matter. What you do differently is put the priorities in order.

If having a relaxing evening with your mom matters, then do what you need to do to make that possible. That would be, doing your homework, your chores, and your practicing BEFORE she gets home from work.

This may be difficult, I get it. So the best way for you to begin making things matter in your life is to begin looking at the benefits.

What is the benefit to doing your homework, practice, and chores, before your mom gets home from work?

_____

What is the benefit of waiting to watch television and play games?

_____

What is the benefit of having everything done by the time mom gets home from work?

_____

What is the benefit of making your mom happy?

_____

What is the benefit of helping out around the house?

_____

Get used to asking the question "What is the benefit to me?" Because there is either going to be a benefit, or a consequence to how you use your time. Every moment matters, and it's up to you to decide why it matters. Here are some practice lines.

The benefit of

_____

now

Is _____ later.

The benefit of

_____

now

Is _____ later.

The benefit of

_____

now

Is _____ later.

16

One of "Those" people

Have you ever met someone who talks a good game, but has nothing to show for it? Have you ever noticed how some people like to talk a lot, but when it comes to taking action, they tend to find an excuse for why not, instead of a reason why?

In my lifetime, I've witnessed this a lot! There are two types of people you will meet in this world. There are the "Talkers" and then there are the "Doers." The doers are the people I'd like you to spend your time with. They are the people who encourage you to take action on the RIGHT things and will even do them with you.

You know what the RIGHT things are. The right things are the things you can tell adults about. A pretty safe rule is that if you wouldn't tell your parents, grandparents and teachers about it....DON'T DO IT!

That's where the talkers tend to come in. The talkers want to TALK you in to doing something that will waste your valuable time. Now that you are starting to understand some of the things I'm sharing with you, I hope you'll start to recognize the talkers.

Talkers are the ones with all the great "Plans" but they never actually make a plan. Doers are the people who take action and want to help you as well.

Talkers TELL you how they are going to do something, and tell you how to do something, but never SHOW you how to do something.

Doers SHOW you how they did something, and TELL you how you could do it even better.

Talkers are the ones who constantly tell you about THEIR BIG PLANS.

Doers are the ones who constantly encourage you and offer help for YOUR BIG PLANS.

The talkers look for the short cut and end up getting nowhere, every time. The doers know exactly where they are going, and if there is no path, they blaze a new trail.

The TALKERS of the world BECOME THE FOLLOWERS of the world, the DOERS of the world BECOME THE LEADERS of the world.

Unless you are going to be completely happy your entire life being told what and how to do something, listening to someone else tell you about their big plans, and following someone else, I SUGGEST BECOMING A DOER!

The doers of the world are the people you see, who don't find excuses, they find a way. They don't look for reasons why not, they look for reasons why they should. They don't look at the challenge, they look for the solution.

Leaders (The Doers) understand there is only one path to success, it's called hard work, focus, and dedication. They set their mind to accomplishing the goal, and they enjoy the journey.

If you find yourself in a situation in life that you don't want to be in, ask yourself this question.

"Who, what, and how am I being that is causing me to have what I don't want?"

This is a VERY important question. When you ask that question, and more importantly answer it honestly, you'll begin to see what you need to BE DOING in order to BEGIN HAVING what you do want!

So if you are "Being" a talker, and nothing is being done, then you need to answer the next question.

"Who, what, and how do I need to be, in order to have what I DO want?"

I'll help you to understand this better in the next chapter.

17

Take a look

Imagine your life, when everyone around you began to take personal responsibility for how their life was going, and how THEY were being. Wouldn't that be AWESOME!

That would mean that each and every person would look at themselves and ask "Who, what, and how am I being that is causing this to happen right now?"

Could you imagine if, instead of blaming you, other people began to see how their behavior was contributing to the situation! WOW! That would be amazing.

My advice, and what I've discovered works, is in EVERY SITUATION, whether it is something you see as good, or bad, ask yourself that question. When you are getting the result you want, then keep doing what you are doing. When you are not getting what you want, stop doing what you are doing.

It really is as simple as that, however, it's not always easy to do. There is a big difference between simple and easy. I like the simple way, however, I don't look for the easy way.

"Who, what, and how am I being?"

That question works, in every situation, for every person, every time. Especially when the answers are honest.

The follow up to that question is "What would I have to BE, in order to have what I want?"

So if you were having an argument, and you asked "Who, what, and how am I being?" because you want to lead the conversation in a new direction. You would (honestly) answer something like "I am being, unwilling to compromise, rude, selfish, and one sided."

Then you would ask, "What would I have to be and do, in order to have what I want?"

Of course (ideally) you would say "I have to be more willing to compromise. I have to listen to what the other person needs. I have to give a little more."

By being willing to look at your own behavior first, and then change your own behavior first, you begin to LEAD the situation.

Wouldn't' it be awesome, if everyone in the world did that! I think it would, which is exactly why I write these books! I want everyone around you to begin taking personal responsibility for how they are treating YOU.

For instance, what if instead of blaming you, your brother or sister looked at how they were being, and what they were doing to cause the argument you were having.

Or, what if your parents stopped yelling and started talking to you like you want to be talked to? Or your teacher began understanding how you need to be treated so you can learn more effectively. Yes, there is an adult version of this book too! Perhaps it's time to mention it to them!

So what can you do, to help yourself, in order to show others what will help you?

You can tell people about this book! You can tell your parents about how much you are enjoying the book. You can tell your friends, or siblings, about how interesting this book is! You can tell your teachers that you think it should be part of your classroom education.

Better yet, if you are BEING A DOER, you would begin to DO what I'm talking about in this book, and then people will begin to ask you. People will begin to ask "Why are you so different (In a good way?) Your friends will begin to appreciate you more. Your parents will begin to appreciate you more. Your teachers will begin to appreciate you more, and when they ask you what you've been doing that is making such a difference, you can say "I'm reading Your Journey Of Being. It's helping me to understand what my J.O.B. is as a young person."

Watch what happens when you begin to behave like a leader, and think, and act like a doer.

Let's use the example of the homework, chores, and instrument practice to illustrate how this works.

Mom gets home from work, and you are stressed out because you didn't do what needed to be done. Now, mom is upset because she is tired, and was hoping today would be different. All she wants to do is have a nice evening with you, but now she is stressed too because she has to make dinner, is upset because your chores aren't done, and instead of enjoying the evening, she is arguing about your homework being done instead.

If this was the case, and YOU were taking personal responsibility for your own life, you would ask "Who, what, and how am I being?"

Honestly, you would say "I am being dishonest with myself and my mom about how I handled my time today. I am being uncaring about my mom, because if I truly cared, I would have done the things I needed to do instead of watching t.v. and playing games. I'm not being true to what matters to me, and I'm being influenced by the distractions around me instead of focusing on my priorities."

Now that is being honest, and taking personal responsibility for your life, don't you think!

So you would say "In order for this to not happen again, I need to be more aware of how the distractions are effecting me negatively. I need to do what needs to be done first, so I can relax and enjoy them completely, later. I need to be thinking of my mom's needs and wants and not just my own."

If you are honest about who, what, and how you are being, the answer to why your life is the way it is, will be clear.

Here are a few practice spaces for you to work on this, the next time you have something in your life that you don't want.

Who, what, and how am I being?

_____

Who, what, and how do I need to be?

_____

Who, what, and how am I being?

_____

Who, what, and how do I need to be?

_____

Who, what, and how am I being?

_____

Who, what, and how do I need to be?

_____

18

Who are they

Who are these people that I'm talking about? Who are your friends? Who are your parents? Who are your teachers? Who is everyone, and what are they doing in your life?

Everyone, and everything in your life is called an "Association." When you "Associate" with something, you spend time with it. So anything you spend time with, you associate with. Got it? Good! You're so smart.

Associations can be people, and they are literally everyone you ever come in contact with. Everyone you associate with is going to have something to do with how your life goes. It may be very small, however, they will all play a role in your life.

Associations can also be non living things, and again, everything you come in contact with is going to have something to do with how your life goes.

Once more, associations are also the places you spend time in. And yes, they play a role in your life.

Associations, can either move you toward the achievement of your goals, or they can keep you away from your goals. So now that you are going to begin being more aware of how the people, places, and things impact your life, I want to ask you a question.

Based on the few goals that you named earlier in this book, what associations are moving you closer to your goals?

Go ahead and write down the people, places, and things that are moving you closer to achieving your goals in life.

_____

_____

_____

Good, now, as difficult as it may be to admit, who and what are the people, places, and things that are keeping you away from achieving your goals?

_____

_____

_____

Did you name any? If you did, excellent! It takes a lot of self reflection to admit when something is holding you back. It's easy to blame something, it's not always easy to admit that you recognize what is holding you back. I want to be perfectly clear about the fact that I don't want you to blame these associations. I simply want you to begin recognizing them.

This is especially difficult when the people are your friends, and sometimes even your family. It's also difficult when the "Things" are what you consider fun. Again, don't get me wrong, I'm not telling you to not have fun, especially if having fun is a goal of yours. You just need to recognize if the "Fun" thing is keeping you from achieving an "Important" thing.

Now that you have recognized some negative associations in your life, how can you begin to spend more time with a positive association?

Again, this takes guts! To be willing to admit that you may need to spend less time with a "Friend" so that you can focus on what matters to you, is not always easy. The good news is, when you begin associating with people who want the same thing as you, new friendships will begin to form. These friendships are the ones that will begin to form the foundation of a lifetime of personal achievement and personal success in your life!

It may also mean associating with the television less, and associating with a book more. It may mean associating with video games less, and associating with a lesson more.

We are constantly in association with something. So it's up to you, to decide what you want to be, and then associate with the people, places, and things that will help you BE IT!

Here is a practice. Fill in the blanks.

In order to live the life I want to live, I will associate with:

_____More and

_____Less

_____More and

_____Less

_____More and

_____Less

If you are one of the rare few people who are willing and able to not only admit what it is going to take, but actually take action on it, then you are going to be one of the greatest leaders in the world!

I like to think of the negative associations in life as the "Energy Zombies!" They are the people who you tend to complain about. They are the people who tend to complain to you. They are the people who are groaning about life, and making their way through each day with that bent over zombie limp.

An energy zombie only has one goal in life. They want to bite your face off.

Okay, maybe not really. However, they do tend to like to use your energy to fuel their desire. Typically, their desire is to do nothing, find a shortcut, or take the "easy way out." Yet, have you ever known a zombie to want to be alone? No way! Zombies love to chase you down, and turn you into a zombie.

What I want to do is give you the weapons it takes to destroy the energy zombies, and the skills it takes to get away from them.

Don't waste your time and energy attempting to turn a "Friend" who is an energy zombie, back into who you think they should be. If you must, lock yourself in your room, and work on your goals. Don't let the zombies in or they will infect you with zombieism!

19

Energy Boosters

Have you begun to identify the energy zombies in your life? Be extra careful, because some of them might be living in your house! They might even have your last name! AAAAHHHH!

In order to have the energy it takes to live the life you want, I'd like to give you a couple quick tips about energy.

At your age, I would guess that energy isn't really an issue. You probably have plenty of it. However, when it comes to achieving your goals, it takes just a bit of FOCUSED energy.

It's actually simple to achieve your goals, it's just a little bit easier not to. I'm going to keep walking you step by step, so I need you to have the energy it takes to keep up. Fair?

Okay, the first thing that can either boost or drain your energy is the people in your life. So if you have identified some energy zombies that you don't want to spend as much time around, then you are going to have to escape somehow.

They don't give up easy, so you have to have energy to get away. You also need a weapon sometimes. In this book, I'm going to give you the best weapon in the world. Words!

Your words are extremely powerful, and can stop a zombie in their tracks. However, if you don't use them correctly, you might make an energy zombie mad. And mad zombies are not a good thing!

So here is an idea of what you can say to an energy zombie who you don't just want to run away from.

"Hey _____! I've been reading this book, and it's encouraging me to

_____.

I really like hanging out (doing what?)

_____

And I love being with you. I just wanted to let you know that I'm going to spend some more time

_____

And that means I won't be (doing what?)

_____

As much. I'd like it if you and I were to do this together, so maybe we could

_____.

What do you think?

Here is an example of how that might sound.

_____

"Hey Mark! I've been reading this book, and it's encouraging me to try out for the varsity football team. I really like hanging out playing video games, And I love being with you. I just wanted to let you know that I'm going to spend some more time focused on being a quarterback, and that means I won't be playing video games as much. I'd like it if you and I were to do this together, so maybe we could play catch for an hour every day. What do you think?

OR

"Hey Jenna, I've been reading this book, and it's encouraging me to Follow my dream of being an artist. I really like hanging out talking and watching videos, and I love being with you. I just wanted to let you know that I'm going to spend some more time drawing and painting, and that means I won't be spending time on YouTube As much. I'd like it if you and I were to do this together, so maybe we could spend an hour each day focused on doing something creative. What do you think?

_____

Go ahead and fill in the blanks if you would like to practice saying that to someone.

This conversation might go one of two ways. Either, they will say "That sounds great!" Or, "What's the book?" Or, "Whatever you are doing, I want to do."

However, it could go the other way too. That person might say "That's stupid!" Or, "Oh, so you don't want to be friends anymore?" Or, "Fine, I'll just go be by myself then if you don't want to be with me."

Of course, there are numerous ways that your association might answer you. It's up to you to decide whether or not you want them to be part of your overall goal, or not. Some people just aren't meant to be in your life for certain things, and you need to be willing to let them go for that part.

This doesn't mean that you need to ditch all your friends, lock yourself in your room, and sit by yourself at lunch. It's simply a suggestion that you begin valuing your time and your energy. Because, at all times people are either taking your time, and taking your energy, or, they are giving you time, and giving you energy.

Then there are things like your physical exercise, and your nutrition that also either drain your energy, or give you energy. My personal suggestion, find something you love to do that requires you to move, actively, for at least a half hour each day. That can even be playing a dance or a sport video game on a body motion detector.

Getting in the habit of moving more, is going to benefit you for your entire life. People get old because they stop moving.

65

I always hear people talking about wanting to "Re-tire." I think to myself, "You're already tired, why do you want to be tired again?"

People typically want to retire, because they are tired of what they are doing. If you can decide, at your age, what you want to be doing, and achieving, during your life time, you will discover new energy every day.

It's a common misunderstanding that people have energy or don't have energy. Instead, we either generate energy, or we don't generate energy.

Your physical movement, your associations and your nutrition, are all things that help you generate energy when you associate with the right ones.

When it comes to nutrition, I encourage you to ask your parents if you can go to www.KidsHealth.org and learn a bunch of great tips to help you eat right so you can have the energy you need to achieve your goals. In fact, that site is a great way for you to learn about many ways to handle life as a young person.

I'd like to finish this section by telling you that the sooner you can begin identifying what helps you to generate energy because it makes you feel ALIVE, the better off you are going to be in life because FEELING ALIVE is a huge part of BEING ALIVE!

Best of all, if you can figure out a way to turn your love of something, into a career, then you won't ever want to retire! You'll want to wake up each day, and jump out of bed to get to work on what is important to you.

That is what living a life of passion and purpose is all about. When you live a life of passion and purpose, based on what you love to do, and who you love to be, you will have a life that is more energized and rewarding than most people on this earth!

The most successful people in the world find a way to combine what makes them feel the most alive, with a way to earn money from it. Regardless of whether or not you believe success is purely financial, it's not. You don't have to be rich to be successful, you just need to feel like you are living your life in the absolute best, and truest way that you feel you were born to live it.

You are made from energy, so by activating what charges your body, you feel energized. That can be anything, and it's different for each person.

Your Journey Of Being A Teenager

Go ahead and write down some ideas of what energizes you! What makes you feel the best?

I feel energized when I am:

_____

_____

_____

67

20

Focommintegrity

Are you ready to truly be one of the people in this world who make a difference? If you are, then these words are something you will want to embrace.

A lot of people are afraid of these words because they can be scary.

Focus is paying attention to what is important and intentionally doing what it takes to reach the point where you have what you want.

Commitment is doing what you said you would do, even after the mood you said it in is gone.

Integrity is doing what you said you would do, how and when you said you would do it, no matter what.

So despite the fact that my grammar teacher wouldn't let me make up my own words in school, I'm going to do it now. Here is my new word:

Focommintegrity: Intentionally Doing what you said you would do, how and when you said you would do it, even if you aren't in the mood, no matter what, because it is important!

Did I lose you? Were you okay with all of this up until this part? If so, stay with me, we'll get through this together!

Focommintegrity is not an easy thing to have. That's why many people don't have it! You have to be willing to do what most people won't do.

Here is the good news! When you are willing to do what most people won't do, you will be able to have what most people don't have!

Look around you from now on. When you see something that stands out, because it's above average, do everything you can to find out HOW the person got that thing.

Ask questions!

If you see someone with the job you want, ask them how they got the job.

If you see someone with the phone you want, ask them how they were able to afford the phone.

If you see someone with the team position you want, ask them how they got the position and what you would need to do to get it.

If you see someone doing something you want to do, ask them how they got to the point where they could do it.

When you get the answer, duplicate what they did! Especially if they got what they have by working to get it, and not just because their parents got it for them. That means they were focused on their goal, they stayed committed to the goal, and they used integrity to achieve the goal. They had Focommintegrity!

The greatest way to achieve success is to find someone who has already done what you want to do, and then do exactly what they did to get it. If you are really lucky, you will form a friendship with that person and they will help you to reach the peak even faster than they did.

When you find someone like that, hang on to every word they say. Their words will be some of the most precious treasures you will ever discover on your journey of being what you want to be!

21

Pointing Fingers

Have you ever pointed the finger of blame at someone? I know I have. Especially before I began to understand how many fingers were pointing back at me.

If you are pointing the finger of blame at someone else, all of your other fingers are pointing back at you!

I'd like to ask you a question.

Who is the most important person in your life?

I'll give you a couple hints:

The most important person in your life is the person who controls your beliefs.

The most important person in your life is the person who controls your actions.

If you haven't guessed it yet, I'll tell you the answer.

The most important person in your life is YOU!

You are the person who controls your life. You are the person who controls your beliefs. You are the person who controls your actions.

You, yes you, are the most important person in your life. There are many other people who are a close second, however, you always come first.

Now, let me clarify what I mean. I'm not telling you to be selfish, only thinking of yourself, and always putting your needs, wants, and desires above everyone else's. That would be the exact opposite of how I suggest you behave and view yourself.

What I am saying is that by always putting yourself first, you take personal responsibility for your life. That is a very rare quality for people to have!

Also, by putting yourself first, you honor yourself because you stand by your own values. Leaders understand that only one person can ever make them do something over the long term….. themselves.

Sure, at this stage of life, you may find yourself in a situation where you aren't able to do exactly what you want to do for yourself. I understand that.

What I'm talking about, when I say to always put yourself first, is to always consider what you want to get out of each and every thought and action in your life.

By focusing on (Intentionally paying attention to) what you think, say, and do, because you want to achieve a certain result, you begin to take control of your life! You begin to CREATE your life, and overcome circumstances, rather than life creating circumstances that make you feel stuck.

Remember, it's YOUR time, it's YOUR belief, it's YOUR action, and it's YOUR result.

If I know one thing about you, I know that you are 100% responsible for your role in your life! Play your part well, and you will be the star of the show!

For instance, when you walk in to a room, are you intentionally being positive, because you are choosing to be positive? Or, do you wait to see how the room will make you feel?

When you go to talk to someone, do you approach the person like they are going to be fun to talk to, and intentionally treat them kindly? Or, do you wait to see how they are going to make you feel?

If you are the new person, do you make it someone else's responsibility to make you feel welcome? Or, do you walk in to the room like you belong there and make other people feel welcome in your presence?

You should, in all situations, be the person responsible for how you feel, act, speak, respond, view, and live in each moment. You should decide before you even get out of bed each day, how you are going to live your life that day. Once you do that, there is no room for finger pointing, because it's your choice.

If you wake up each day and say "I'm going to make this a great day! I'm going to be happy, positive, thankful, kind, generous, caring, thoughtful," and anything else you want to be, then BE IT!!

Things will do their best to stop you, but it's up to you to use all your fingers to climb over, get around, or dig under what gets in your way. Don't point the finger of blame for how your life goes at anyone else!

What are some ways you've been pointing fingers? Who do you tend to put the blame on? What do you say is the reason you can't, or won't do something? It's time to give it up!

I'm going to stop _____

And I will start _____

I'm going to stop _____

And I will start _____

I'm going to stop _____

And I will start _____

I'm going to stop _____

And I will start _____

21

Conscuitionally Conscintentional

Are you familiar with Jimini Cricket? If not, I'll tell you who he is. Jimini is the little cricket in the animated film Pinocchio. His advice was simple "Always let your conscience be your guide."

How do you do that if you don't know what your conscience is? Well, I'm going to tell you, so if you don't want to know, don't read this section. Just kidding...please read it.

Your conscience is that little voice in your head that tells you when you are about to do something that you shouldn't, or that you've just done something that you shouldn't have done. It's the feeling of guilt, the shame of the action, and the thought that warns you of the choice you are about to make. It typically comes up in the decision making process, and you can either ignore it, or honor it's advice.

Your conscience lives in your head. So does your intuition.

Your intuition is similar to your conscience in that your intuition uses past reference points, based on prior results, to intelligently predict future results.

Does all this sound complicated and scientific? That's because it is. But don't worry, I'm not going to make you dissect a brain. Sorry to all those who think that would be cool.

Stay with me here, because I want to give you some REALLY useful stuff.

Not like that pesky homework that just fills your head with useless information. Please don't tell your teachers I said that, I still have nightmares of being in school in my underwear and I don't need any teachers mad at me.

Okay, two more big words here. They are similar to the other two, so pay attention! If you've been sleep reading, please wake up now!

The first word is conscious. Conscious means that you are aware of what is going on.

The next word is Intentional. Intentional means to do it on purpose.

Now, you know I love to play with words. So I'm going to give you a couple of words that most of the world doesn't use. Probably because they aren't real words......yet. But I'm working on helping the world understand me.

Here you go.

Conscuitionally Conscintentional

What the heck? Is that even legal? To take two words and just group them together? Actually I'm writing this from my jail cell, so apparently not. Just kidding of course, I'm on my couch.

Here are my completely made up words and my completely made up definitions of each of those fake words.

Conscintentional – Being aware on purpose.

Conscuitional – Making the choice because you believe you will get the result you want.

So if you are being aware of the choice you are making because you believe you want to achieve a certain result on purpose, you are being Conscuitionally Conscintentional! You could also say that you are being Conscintentionally Conscuitional if it's easier for you!

Again, most people don't use it, not conscuintenionally anyway. Most people aren't aware that the choices they make serve a purpose.

The fact is, EVERYTHING you do serves a purpose. So that also means that everything you SAY serves a purpose.

With that understood (By the way, adults won't understand these big words so don't explain it to them) I want you to get used to making your choices conscintentionally from now on so you stand out from the crowd and become a leader.

Of course in order to become a leader who makes good choices, you'll need to make those choices based on your conscuition.

That means that you will need to be fully aware and intentionally making your choices based on that little voice in your head that tells you what you should be doing, based on your previous results, so you can intelligently achieve the future results you desire!

Got it? Good! See, this is way too simple for adults to understand.

To give you an example, I'll use an example.

If your friends are all doing something that you conscintentionally know you should not be doing, what should you do? You should conscuitionally not do it, and then get out of the situation.

That is what a leader does.

If you make the conscuitional choice to do it anyway, you are going against your conscintention, and you will probably experience a result that hopefully will lead you to make a better choice next time. This is also known as punishment, consequence, and in some cases (as you get older) jail time. This time, I'm not kidding!

That is what a follower does.

Don't be a follower!

If I've confused you, I'm sorry about that. Feel free to read this, and any section for that matter, again. The more you understand each section of the book, the better the next book in this series will be.

The most important thing is to keep going! I have more to teach you so that I can fill some more pages of another book. Stick with me, and take a break if you need to. I'll be here when you are ready to keep moving toward the peak, where all of this stuff will make complete sense.

I write this way Conscintentionally. I also write Conscuitionally because I believe you will get the results you want if I do.

Plus, if I use words that adults won't understand, then it can be like our own secret code words for why you are doing what you are doing! Most adults don't understand why we behave the way we do.

Hey, I can still be young if I choose to be!

22

C.H.O.I.C.E.

You probably hear me using two words quite often. They are decision, and choice. I want to clarify what the difference is for you.

A decision, is something that can be altered over and over again. You make decisions in your head. They don't really have much of an effect on your life.

A choice however, is something that you make one time. You make a choice, that choice makes you take an action, and that action produces a result. The result allows for a new moment of decision and then a choice, action, result. It's a constant cycle.

You can spend a long time deciding what to do. Choices however, happen in an instant and they alter the course of your life.... instantaneously.

For instance, you decide whether or not to say something, then you choose to say it.

You can also decide what shirt to wear, then you choose to put it on.

You can also decide what you want to eat, then you choose to eat it.

I would like to help you make the right choices in life by offering you another acronym.

C.H.O.I.C.E.

Choice, is an acronym that you can use to remember most of what you've learned (or not learned) in this book.

The "C" stands for Consistency. If you remember, consistency is the real determining factor in how quickly you get what you want, and how often or long you have what you have. On your journey toward the peak, it's important that you remain consistent! So choose, right now, to BE CONSISTENT!

If you have been consistently doing something that is not getting you the result you want, make the choice to change your behavior. Consistently do something else, and see what happens!

If you are consistently getting bad grades, then you are consistently doing what results in bad grades.

If you are consistently arguing with your parents, you (and they of course) are consistently doing what results in an argument.

The "H" stands for Honest. When you are deciding what matters to you, who your associations should be, and what choice you need to make, you need to be honest with yourself and with others. Honesty is not just something that is related to telling the truth. Honesty is something that must be part of who you are at your core. Choose to BE HONEST!

If you aren't getting the results you want, you need to be honest with yourself about why. Most people have a hard time being honest, especially when it comes to accepting personal responsibility for how their life is turning out. Don't be most people! Be honest with yourself!

For instance, if you are yelling, then you need to be honest with yourself. Is yelling going to get you the conversation you want?

If you are watching television, instead of studying, is watching television going to get you the grades that you want?

"O" stands for Open. Being open, means that you are open to the possibility that something else may exist. That may be a new way of doing something, a different and possibly better point of view, and even being open to suggestions. When you are open, you allow new beliefs into your life. As long as those beliefs are in line with your core values, then go ahead and allow them in. You can change your beliefs in an instant, so be sure they are in line with the results you want. Choose to BE OPEN. That includes being open minded, open hearted, and open armed.

If someone is asking you to do something, be open to the possibility that it might benefit you.

If someone wants to love you more, be open to accepting their love.

If you don't agree with something someone says, be open minded to the possibility that there are other ways of seeing the world.

Integrity is the "I" in c.h.o.i.c.e. and it's important because when you do what you said you would do, how and when you said you would do it, even when you don't feel like it, people trust you. Trust is something that is earned and lost easily. Integrity keeps trust alive. If you want to live a life where people trust you, and you are looked at in a great way, BE INTEGRITOUS. Yes I made up that word too. It means to live with integrity.

If you make a promise, keep it!

If someone is counting on you for something, do it!

If there is a way that something is supposed to be done, do it that way!

Living the life you want to live, and achieving your goals, requires Commitment to living a life in the pursuit of excellence. The "C" is commitment. You must BE COMMITTED to living the life you want to live. No one else can live your life for you, and no one else can get you the results that you want. So commit to yourself! After all, you are the most important person in your life.

If you commit to exercising every day, because losing weight, or being healthy matters to you, then be committed to it!

If you want to be a good friend, then be committed to your friends!

If you set a goal, and you are determined to achieve that goal, then be committed to that goal, no matter what!

Finally, it may sound weird to say it this way, however, I want to encourage you to BE ENERGY! By being energy, you are making the choice to BE ENERGIZED! In scientific terms, you are just one big bundle of energy anyway. How you choose to BE, is going to have a direct result on how energized you feel, appear, act, and experience life. If you are living your life, doing the things you need to do, in order to have the things you want to have, your energy levels will be off the charts!

If you walk into a room, choose to BE positive energy!

If you are talking to someone, choose to BE energized by what they are saying.

When you wake up in the morning, choose what energy you are going to give off. Be happy energy! Be caring energy! Be loving energy! Be understanding energy!

You get to make the choice of who, what, and how you are being in every moment of your life. What you choose to be, is going to directly reflect what you do, and ultimately what you have.

Be what you were born to be! In every moment of your life, ask yourself, "In this moment, what do I need to be in order to live the life I want to live?" then BE WHAT YOU NEED TO BE, in order to DO WHAT YOU NEED TO DO, so you can HAVE WHAT YOU WANT TO HAVE!

IT'S ALL A CHOICE OF WHO, WHAT, AND HOW YOU WANT TO BE!

Enjoying the journey so far? If so, I'd love to invite you to continue to climb higher, toward the peak of what's possible for your life. The next book in this series is called:

Your Journey Of Being a Teenager – The Next Level.

The Next Level will help you to fully understand how that little voice in our head affects EVERYTHING we experience in life! Once you finish reading that book, your life will be better than you can possibly imagine, because you'll see life from a whole new perspective!

Notes

_____

_____

_____

_____

_____

_____

_____

_____

_____

_____

_____

_____

_____

_____

_____

_____

_____

_____

Notes

_____

_____

_____

_____

_____

_____

_____

_____

_____

_____

_____

_____

_____

_____

_____

_____

_____

_____

_____

_____

_____

Notes

_____

_____

_____

_____

_____

_____

_____

_____

_____

_____

_____

_____

_____

_____

_____

_____

_____

_____

_____

_____

_____

_____

_____

Notes

Notes

_____

_____

_____

_____

_____

_____

_____

_____

_____

_____

_____

_____

_____

_____

_____

_____

_____

_____

_____

_____

_____

_____

Made in the USA
Charleston, SC
09 December 2016